M

Gideon v. Wainwright

Free Legal Counsel

For my husband,
Peter Karoczkai,
with love

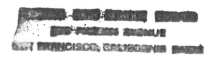

M

Gideon v. Wainwright
Free Legal Counsel

Victoria Sherrow

Landmark Supreme Court Cases

Enslow Publishers, Inc.

40 Industrial Road   PO Box 38
Box 398   Aldershot
Berkeley Heights, NJ 07922   Hants GU12 6BP
USA   UK

http://www.enslow.com

2005304

Library of Congress Cataloging-In-Publication Data

Sherrow, Victoria.
    Gideon v. Wainwright: free legal counsel / Victoria Sherrow.
       p. cm. — (Landmark Supreme Court Cases)
    Includes bibliographical references and index.
    ISBN 0-89490-507-4
    1. Gideon, Clarence Earl—Trials, litigation, etc.
—Juvenile literature. 2. Wainwright, Louie L.—Trials,
litigation, etc.—Juvenile literature. 3. Right to counsel
—United States—Juvenile literature. 4. United States.
Supreme Court—Juvenile literature.
    [1. Right to counsel.] I. Title. II. Series.
KF228.G53S53 1994
345.73'056—dc20   93-45981
[347.30556]   CIP
                          AC
Printed in the United States of America

10 9 8 7 6 5

Photo Credits: Collection of the Supreme Court of the United States, p. 24;
Courtesy of the Archives of the Supreme Court of the United States, pp. 58, 65,
68, 81; Florida State Archives, pp. 12, 29; Florida State Archives: Woody Wisner,
p. 9; Franz Jantzen, "Collection of the Supreme Court of the United States", pp.
48, 53; Harris & Ewing, "Collection of the Supreme Court of the United States",
p. 36; National Archives, p. 33.

Cover Photos: Franz Jantzen, "Collection of the Supreme Court of the United
States" (background); Franz Jantzen "Collection of the Supreme Court of the
United States" (inset).

Contents

1

Prisoner #003826

From time to time throughout history, individuals have taken actions that have the capacity to dramatically affect society. Some of these people have been among the rich and powerful, the brilliant or well-educated, effecting change through their positions or talents. Others have been unknown or ordinary citizens pursuing a cause they believed in.

Acting on his own during the early 1960s, a poor, middle-aged man named Clarence Earl Gideon set out to right a situation he felt was wrong. In his case, Gideon felt he had been unfairly convicted of a crime and had not received a fair trial. At the time he sought a remedy, Gideon was not thinking about making history; he just wanted to prove his point and get out of prison.

Gideon's struggle to change the law began in 1961. Then fifty years old, he was arrested and charged with breaking into the Bay Harbor Poolroom with the intent to commit burglary, a felony in Florida. Gideon protested that he was innocent. On August 4, 1961, he found himself on trial in a Panama City, Florida, courtroom. If he were convicted, he could spend several years in jail.

Clarence Gideon was indigent (without money) and had only an eighth-grade education. Nevertheless, he had tried to read and understand the law before he went to court. As his trial began, Judge Robert L. McCrary of the fourteenth Judicial Circuit addressed Gideon, the defendant, and asked, "Are you ready to go to trial?"[1] "I am not ready, your Honor," replied Gideon.[2]

The judge expressed his surprise. He asked the defendant why he was not prepared since he knew he was going to be put on trial for breaking and entering the poolroom.

The slightly built, white-haired Gideon offered a brief explanation: "I have no Counsel."[3]

The judge then asked Gideon if he had known his trial was scheduled for that day; Gideon admitted that he had. "Why, then," asked Judge McCrary, "did you not secure Counsel and be prepared to go to trial?"[4]

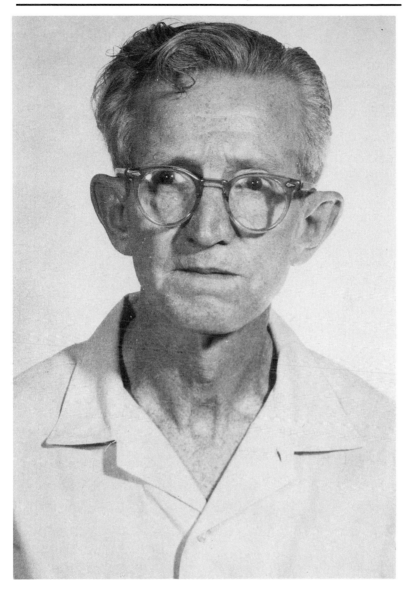

Clarence Earl Gideon, shown here, was a man of slight build and white hair. Little did he know that his insistence that the court provide him with an attorney to represent him in his case would change the face of our legal system.

Gideon's answer was simple: He had no money to pay an attorney. He walked up to the bench and stood before the judge, saying softly, "I request this Court to appoint counsel to represent me in this trial."[5]

"Mr. Gideon, I am sorry, but I cannot appoint counsel to represent you in this case," said Judge McCrary. He told Gideon that under Florida law, a state only provided free legal counsel when a poor defendant was charged with a capital crime, such as murder.[6]

Gideon was confused. He had read the Sixth Amendment to the Constitution and knew almost all the words by heart. The Amendment guarantees that every American shall enjoy the right to "a speedy and public trial," among other things. At the end, it says that a person who is accused of a crime shall have the right to "have the assistance of counsel for his defense."[7]

Besides that, Gideon believed that a section of the Fourteenth Amendment to the Constitution meant people had the right to an attorney. The Amendment says that citizens shall not be deprived "of life, liberty, or property without due process of law."[8] To Gideon, the words "due process of law" meant legal representation in his trial, as would be available to someone who could afford to hire an attorney. He was convinced he could not have a fair trial without the aid of a lawyer.[9] Based on his reading of the Constitution, Gideon insisted to Judge McCrary, "The United States Supreme Court says I am entitled to be represented by counsel."[10]

In the end, the judge did not appoint a lawyer to assist Clarence Gideon. The court noted that Gideon had asked it to appoint an attorney for him but "the Court denied the request, and informed the Defendant that the only time the Court could appoint Counsel was in cases where the Defendant was charged with a capital offense."[11]

Gideon had been mistaken about the law. The Supreme Court had never said that people in his predicament had the right to a court-appointed attorney—in fact, the Court had said something different as recently as 1942. Only people in specified circumstances were eligible to have free counsel, and Gideon did not fit any of those conditions.

The words of the Constitution convinced Gideon that he had certain rights. But it is the United States Supreme Court that interprets those words and applies them to situations in everyday life. A famous Justice on the Court during the 1920s said, "We are under a Constitution, but the Constitution is what the Court says it is."[12] Although Justice Charles Evans Hughes

The Florida State Penitentiary at Raiford would become Clarence Gideon's home when he was sentenced to five years there as prisoner #003826. It was there that he began studying law books at the prison library, searching for a way to convince the Supreme Court that even without the money to pay for one, he was still entitled to a lawyer—and a fair trial.

was exaggerating, there is much truth in what he said. In 1942, the Court had heard *Betts* v. *Brady*, a case similar to Gideon's. A majority of Justices—six to three—had held that states need not provide attorneys for poor defendants in noncapital crimes.

After trying to defend himself in the Panama City courtroom, Clarence Earl Gideon was found guilty of burglary and sentenced to five years in the Florida State Penitentiary at Raiford. Now Prisoner #003826, he stubbornly refused to accept the idea that he had not been entitled to a lawyer. Gideon began studying the law books in the prison library, reading hours every day in his cell. He searched for a way to convince the highest court in the land that a defendant who had no money still needed a lawyer in order to have a fair trial.

Since beginning its work in 1790, the Supreme Court has preferred not to overrule previous decisions, although it occasionally does so. So Gideon faced a daunting task. A poorly educated high school dropout, he must now try to understand complicated laws and fulfill the requirements necessary before the nine Justices would consider his case. Spending hours bent over books in the prison library and writing in his cell at Raiford, Clarence Gideon struggled to complete a written petition asking the highest court in the land to review his trial and conviction.

2

The Rights of the Accused

We, the People of the United States, in Order to form a more perfect Union, establish Justice, insure domestic Tranquility, provide for the common defense, promote the general Welfare, and secure the Blessings of Liberty to ourselves and our Posterity, do ordain and establish this Constitution for the United States of America.

The Preamble to the United States Constitution shows that the framers of the Constitution intended to "establish justice." Throughout that document, particularly in the Bill of Rights (first ten amendments to the Constitution), it is clear that the men who drafted it cared about the rights of people accused of a crime. They viewed such persons as innocent until proven guilty. They set up a framework of safeguards for such defendants.

It is no wonder. The nation's founders were familiar with European countries where such rights were often nonexistent or ignored. In some places, laws were written by ruling nobles and kings and changed at their whims. People accused of a crime might be executed without a trial. When a trial was held, it was sometimes in secret, or decisions were made by judges who had been chosen by hereditary, not elected, rulers. Trial by jury was not a universal right. In addition, people might have their property seized by the government without just cause or the right to any legal remedy.

These conditions, although hard to imagine today, existed in numerous countries during the 1700s when the United States Constitution was written. Such conditions offended James Madison, Thomas Jefferson, Benjamin Franklin, and others among the nation's "Founding Fathers." They sought a form of government in which every American could enjoy equal justice under the law.

The rights of criminal defendants were discussed and debated by the framers, then written into the Fifth, Sixth, and Eighth Amendments to the Constitution in 1791. Many people are familiar with part of the Fifth Amendment, having heard the phrase "I take the Fifth" or "I refuse to answer on the grounds that I may tend to incriminate myself." A portion of the actual amendment reads:

> No person shall be held to answer for a capital or otherwise infamous crime, unless on a presentment or indictment of a Grand Jury, except in cases arising in the land or naval forces, or in the militia . . . nor shall any person be subject for the same offense to be twice put in jeopardy of life or limb; nor shall be compelled in any criminal case to be a witness against himself nor be deprived of life, liberty, or property, without due process of law; nor shall private property be taken for public use without just compensation.

Among other things, this amendment protects people from being brought to trial for a serious crime unless a grand jury has first determined that the crime was committed, and, second, that the accused probably did it. The law also states that the government cannot execute or imprison somebody without following certain prescribed methods of the law.

The Sixth Amendment discusses the right of the accused to a fair trial. Here, the wording goes:

> In all criminal prosecutions, the accused shall enjoy the right to a speedy and public trial, by an impartial jury of the state and district wherein the crime shall have been committed; which district shall have been previously ascertained by law, and to be informed of the nature and cause of the accusation; to be confronted with the witnesses against him; to have

compulsory process for obtaining witnesses in his favor, and to have the assistance of counsel in his defense.

According to this amendment, people arrested on a federal charge have certain rights, including a public trial as soon as possible after the time of arrest. A jury of fair-minded peers, usually twelve in number, who live near the place of the alleged crime, are supposed to listen to the evidence and deliver a verdict. People standing trial are also provided with the information needed to plan a defense; they have the opportunity to hear, see, and challenge witnesses who testify against them.

The last phrase—"and to have the assistance of counsel in his defense"—is what prompted Clarence Gideon to think the state must be obligated to supply him with an attorney, since he could not afford one himself. It is not difficult to see how he might have interpreted the words this way or to imagine he was unaware that the Supreme Court had applied this amendment only to federal cases, not every kind of criminal case in all the states.

The Eighth Amendment, which also applies in criminal matters, is brief:

Excessive bail shall not be required, nor excessive fines imposed, nor cruel and unusual punishments inflicted.

18

As a result of this amendment, people who have been arrested may often return to their homes or jobs to await trial, after first "putting up" bail (money or property they will have to forfeit if they fail to show up for their trial). Bail is permitted unless defendants are viewed as a danger to society or if the court has strong reasons to believe they will not return for their trial. The last section of the amendment protects people from being tortured or punished excessively for the type of crime committed. For example, the police are not allowed to beat someone they have arrested in order to get a confession, nor can people legally be put to death for petty theft.

The Fourteenth Amendment, Section 1, adopted in 1868, has also come to apply to the rights of criminal defendants, among other things. This amendment was written after the Civil War, its main goal being to protect former slaves. The first clause guarantees that all citizens living in any part of the United States have the same rights as any others. It says:

> All persons born or naturalized in the United States and subject to the jurisdiction thereof, are citizens of the United States and of the state wherein they reside.

The next clause, which has come to be extremely important in modern Constitutional law, says:

No state shall make or enforce any law which shall abridge the privileges or immunities of citizens of the United States; nor shall any state deprive any person of life, liberty, or property, without due process of law; nor deny to any person within its jurisdiction the equal protection of the laws.

In earlier years, the Fifth, Sixth, and Eighth Amendments were considered by the Supreme Court as it grappled with criminal cases. Since the 1900s, the Court has also sometimes cited the Fourteenth Amendment to support various decisions. In asking the Florida judge to supply an attorney for him, Clarence Gideon thought this Amendment applied to his situation, too. He believed that "due process of law" meant he should have access to an attorney, as a wealthier person would have, in the face of possible imprisonment (a deprivation of liberty). But as of 1961 when Gideon was tried, the Supreme Court had not established such a precedent.

What had the Court ruled as of that time? Until the 1930s, the Court had interpreted the Sixth Amendment's "right . . . to have assistance of counsel for his defense" to mean that a person had the right to hire a lawyer for his trial. The wording of the Amendment was such that the Court had much leeway in deciding how to interpret it; the wording permitted defendants to hire attorneys but said nothing about a governmental duty to provide them.

That was until a notorious case in Alabama in 1932 caught the Court's attention. In this case, *Powell* v. *Alabama*, two white girls accused a group of nine black men (also known as the case of the Scottsboro Boys) of raping them while they were hitching a ride on a freight train from Chattanooga to Huntsville, Alabama. In Jackson County, Alabama, a sheriff arrested the nine young men. No evidence of rape was found, but all the defendants were charged with criminal assault and ordered to stand trial. These defendants were all under twenty-one years of age and uneducated; all claimed they were innocent.

When the case reached the Supreme Court, the convictions were reversed by a majority of 7 to 2. In his decision, Justice George Sutherland wrote:

> In a capital case, where the defendant is unable to employ counsel, and is incapable adequately of making his own defense because of ignorance, feeblemindedness, illiteracy, or the like, it is the duty of the court, whether requested or not, to assign counsel for him as a necessary requisite of due process of law. . . . [it would not be sufficient to appoint a lawyer] at such a time or under such circumstances as to preclude the giving of effective aid in the preparation and trial of the case.[1]

Powell v. *Alabama* took a slightly broader view of

the rights of criminal defendants in regard to the Sixth and Fourteenth Amendments. Now, certain kinds of defendants—those who were too poor to hire an attorney as well as too mentally handicapped or helpless to conduct their own defense—were entitled to court-appointed counsel.* The Court cited the Due Process Clause of the Fourteenth Amendment in its ruling, noting that this Amendment protects against violations of individual rights by the states.

The Court went a bit further in 1938 when it decided the case of *Johnson v. Zerbst*. Here, it decided that an indigent criminal defendant was also entitled to have counsel in federal cases and in those involving the death penalty.[2] Justice Hugo L. Black wrote the Court's opinion. The Alabama-born Justice, who would later figure prominently in the *Gideon* case, was one of the staunchest supporters of the "incorporation doctrine"—the idea that all the other rights in the Bill of Rights are meant to be incorporated in the

---

* During their second trial, the Scottsboro defendants were represented by counsel but were again convicted, even though one of the girls who had accused them of assaulting her admitted she had lied. The woman, Ruby Bates, later went to the White House to ask that the men be freed. The Supreme Court considered the case once again in 1935 and overturned it, this time because qualified black people had been prevented from serving on the jury. Finally, the Scottsboro defendants were paroled or released after the charges against them were dropped.[3]

Fourteenth Amendment, and, thus, applied to every state.

After the 1930s, many legal thinkers believed that the rulings in *Powell* v. *Alabama* and *Johnson* v. *Zerbst* meant that the Supreme Court favored the right to an attorney in any criminal trial. Their reading of these cases led them to assume that the Court thought due process of law required this duty on the part of the government.

That did not prove to be true. In *Betts* v. *Brady*, a 1942 case, a man accused of robbery and unable to afford an attorney petitioned the Supreme Court after his conviction. The Court declared that the states did not have an obligation to provide indigent people with attorneys in every case. Speaking for the majority of six, Justice Owen Roberts wrote, ". . . in the great majority of states, it has been the considered judgment of the people, their representatives, and their courts that appointment of counsel is not a fundamental right essential to a fair trial."[4] Reluctant to impose a universal obligation on all the states, the Court commented, "That which may, in one setting, constitute a denial of fundamental fairness, shocking to the universal sense of justice, may, in other circumstances, and in the light of other considerations, fall short of such denial."[5]

Justice Hugo L. Black, shown here in his office at the Supreme Court of the United States, wrote the opinion in the 1938 *Johnson* v. *Zerbst* case. It declared that an indigent criminal defendant was entitled to have an attorney in federal cases and those involving the death penalty.

Justice Black wrote a dissent (contrary opinion), which two other Justices joined. Black called the right to counsel "fundamental," saying, "Any other practice seems to me to defeat the promise of our democratic society to provide equal justice under the law."[6] As a practical matter, Black also pointed out that it was not truly possible to determine someone's innocence or guilt "from a trial in which, as here, denial of counsel has made it impossible to conclude, with any satisfactory degree of certainty, that the defendant's case was adequately presented."[7]

Betts v. *Brady* was still "good law"—in other words, it had not been overturned—when Clarence Gideon was convicted in 1961. Clearly, by the 1960s, the legal system was more intricate than ever, far more complicated than when the Constitution was written in the late 1700s. The rules governing arrests, convictions, and the presentation of evidence at trial had grown in number and complexity. Even well-educated people found it hard to understand the ins and outs of the legal system. For many Americans, it was routine to use lawyers in buying property, signing contracts, and making wills, among other things.

Several Justices on the Court were acutely aware of these trends in society and the increasing use of attorneys for things much less momentous than a criminal trial. Since his dissent in the *Betts* case, Hugo Black had been eager to overturn that decision and continued to promote the idea among his colleagues. His supporters included William O. Douglas, appointed to the Court in 1939, and William Brennan, appointed in 1952.

In addition, a new Chief Justice, Earl Warren, had been appointed to the Court in 1953. The Warren Court had already made sweeping changes in the law, as when it banned government or state-sponsored school segregation in the famous 1954 case, *Brown* v. *Board of Education*. Warren had made it known to the law clerks who screened the petitions mailed to the Court that he would like an appropriate case in which to overturn the decision in *Betts*. One clerk said that "the Chief" had told them to "keep your eyes peeled for a right to counsel case."[8]

On January 8, 1962, a petition arrived at the offices of the Supreme Court, handwritten by a prison inmate named Clarence Gideon.

3

A "Jailhouse Lawyer" Pleads His Case

Clarence Gideon became an inmate at Raiford State Prison in late August, 1961. It was not the first time Gideon had been in trouble with the law or served time in jail. During his fifty-one years he had gone through hard times and been arrested for other noncapital offenses.

Born in Hannibal, Missouri, in 1910, Clarence Earl Gideon was later to describe his childhood as "miserable."[1] When he was fourteen, he quit school and became a drifter. Within a year, he was arrested for stealing some clothing from a store and placed in a juvenile reformatory for three years. Afterwards, he worked in a shoe factory and was married, the first of three times. During the Great Depression he was often out of work and was again arrested for burglary and sent to prison for three years. Once released, he had trouble finding steady work and viewed himself as an "outcast."[2] He was in and out of jail for petty thievery and survived a bout of tuberculosis (also known as TB, an infectious disease of the lungs). By 1960, Gideon had to support six children and a wife who was suffering from alcoholism. He joined a local church, hoping this would help his wife and provide moral training for his children.[3] Gideon's tuberculosis flared up again just as his wife seemed to be recovering. The family relied on their welfare payments of $10 a week to buy food as Gideon underwent lung surgery for the second time. In ill health, he had trouble keeping a steady job.

On June 3, 1961, Gideon was arrested, charged with breaking and entering the Bar Harbor Poolroom and stealing beer, soft drinks, and coins from the vending machine. Under Florida law, this crime was a felony. Gideon told police that he had taken part in poker games at the poolroom but denied having been there at the time the burglary was committed. While admitting that he had committed crimes in the past, Gideon insisted that this time he was innocent.

Nevertheless, he was convicted after trying to

Gideon's cell block at Raiford prison, his new home when he was convicted after unsuccessfully trying to defend himself without an attorney. The small cell became a place of learning. Gideon began to study the books in the prison's library—not an easy task for a man with limited education. His belief that an injustice had been done to him kept him going.

defend himself, without the help of an attorney during
the trial. At Raiford, Gideon began studying the law
books in the prison library. It was an arduous task for
someone with his limited education, but Gideon
persisted. He was driven by a sense of injustice and
later said, "I knew the Constitution guaranteed me a
fair trial, but I didn't see how a man could get one
without a lawyer to defend him."[4]

Gideon's first attempt to gain his release was to sue
out a writ of habeas corpus (that is, send out a written
order) against H. G. Cochran, Jr., the Director of the
Department of Corrections, directing Cochran to
release Gideon from what he considered to be unlawful
imprisonment. Florida law permitted a convicted
person to challenge the constitutionality of his
conviction by petitioning the state supreme court to
issue such a writ. The Florida Supreme Court refused
his request. That left Gideon with one last resort: the
United States Supreme Court.

Would the Supreme Court accept his case?
Although some Justices, including Chief Earl Warren,
were interested in the issue of providing attorneys for
indigent defendants, that was no guarantee that the
Court would consider Clarence Gideon's plea. The
nation's highest court today agrees to hear only about
125 to 150 cases out of the six thousand to seven

thousand that it receives each year for review. Potential litigants (people bringing the lawsuit) must meet stiff requirements in order to qualify. They must print or type their documents clearly on non-see-through paper and file forty copies of their petitions. The Court also has a great deal of discretion in deciding which cases it will hear. A petitioner must file a request for a writ of certiorari, a formal request that the Court will review the actions of the lower court, in this case the Florida court that had convicted Gideon. The Court then decides whether to grant the writ and review that particular case.

Before granting a writ, four of the nine Justices have to agree that the Court should consider the case in question. Cases that involve an important federal constitutional issue or federal law are most likely to be heard. The Court may also choose to hear cases that will give them an opportunity to expand upon or overturn a previous decision. In presenting his case, Clarence Gideon was to contend that it involved constitutional questions in regard to the Sixth Amendment "assistance of counsel" and the Due Process Clause of the Fourteenth Amendment. Although Gideon was unaware of it, his case also would entail reexamining the 1942 case of *Betts* v. *Brady*.

31

Gideon set out to write a petition to the Supreme Court asking it to overturn his conviction. Because he had no attorney to help him and lacked the $100 filing fee, Gideon filed what is called an *in forma pauperis* (I.F.P.) petition. This kind of petition enables poor defendants to file on their own, without the help of an attorney or the payment of the fee. In it, he claimed that the Florida court's refusal to appoint counsel for him denied rights "guaranteed by the Constitution and the Bill of Rights by the United States Government."[5] Painstakingly, in pencil, he wrote about his case on lined prison paper in what one observer has called "schoolboy-style printed script."[6] He used the legal terms he had discovered while reading books from the prison library.

Gideon later told author Anthony Lewis, who visited him at Raiford Prison, about how hard it had been to understand how to submit his legal petition correctly: "The Supreme Court sent me a book of rules, but I still can't understand them. The rules take a pretty educated man to figure them out."[7] Despite these obstacles, Gideon gained a reputation for his legal know-how. Soon, other inmates were asking the advice of this "jailhouse lawyer" as they tried to appeal their own cases.

Gideon mailed his petition. When it arrived on

In the Supreme Court of the United States
Washington D.C
Motion for leave to proceed in Forma Pauperis
Clarence Earl Gideon, Petitioner
vs.
H. G. Cochran Jr, Director, Divisions of corrections State of Florida Respondent

Petitioner, Clarence Earl Gideon, who is now held in the Florida state penitentiary, asks leave to file the attached petition for a Writ of Certiorari to the United States Supreme Court, directed to the Supreme Court of the State of Florida, without prepayment of costs and to proceed in Forma Pauperis. The petitioner's affidavit in support is attached hereto.

Clarence Earl Gideon
counsel for Petitioner

Affidavit in support of petition for leave to proceed in Forma Pauperis
Clarence Earl Gideon, petitioner
vs.
H. G. Cochran Jr, Director, Divisions of corrections State of Florida, Respondent.

I Clarence Earl Gideon, being duly sworn according to law, depose and say that I am

Page one of Gideon's petition to the Supreme Court is shown here. Because he lacked the one-hundred-dollar filing fee, he was able to file a special kind of petition. Written in pencil on lined prison paper, Gideon's petition caught the eye of Chief Justice Earl Warren's law clerk. The clerk was under instructions to look for a case involving the "free legal counsel" issue.

January 8, 1962, Chief Justice Earl Warren's law clerk opened it, along with other I.F.P petitions. After reviewing it, the clerk wrote a memo and attached it to the envelope containing the petition. Each Justice received a copy of the memo and petition before the group met in June of 1962 to discuss the case.

Only one Justice, Tom C. Clark, disagreed with the other eight about Gideon's case. The others answered "yes" to the question of whether the Court should reconsider their decision in *Betts* v. *Brady*. Justice John M. Harlan wrote on his clerk's memo, "I think the time has come when we should meet the *Betts* question head on."[8]   In the meantime, the State of Florida answered a letter from the Supreme Court asking it to respond to Gideon's petition. The state's attorney general and his assistant sent a thirteen-page response in which they justified their decision not to provide Gideon with counsel at his 1961 burglary trial. Most of their reasoning was based on the Court's ruling in the *Betts* case.

After reading his copy of the State's response, Clarence Gideon was unsure how to respond. He again wrote to the Supreme Court, claiming that his limited knowledge of the law and lack of access to many law books left him unable to answer all the complex arguments made by the "learned Attorney General of

Florida." Expressing his basic disagreement with the state's argument, he said that he intended "to show this Court that a citizen of the State of Florida cannot get a just and fair trial without the aid of counsel."[9]

That June, after hearing that his case had been selected for review by the Supreme Court, Gideon wrote asking them to appoint an attorney to represent him in those proceedings. It was the Court's custom to provide an attorney for all litigants too poor to hire one. At Chief Justice Earl Warren's suggestion, the Justices chose Abe Fortas, a highly respected Washington, D.C., attorney. Fortas was regarded as a brilliant legal scholar and leader in the District of Columbia legal community. A colleague said of him, "He's the lawyer's lawyer, the brain surgeon, the guy you call in when all else fails."[10] Fortas agreed to represent Clarence Gideon. The Court asked Fortas to prepare a case in which he argued for a reconsideration of the *Betts* decision. Yet as Fortas began to work with Gideon, he faced some difficult choices. He had a moral obligation to represent the best interests of his client—namely, to have Gideon's conviction set aside. He wondered whether there was some way to show that Gideon did qualify for legal help in his trial, based on the special circumstances (for example, feeble-mindedness, illiteracy, mental illness) that would

Abe Fortas, a highly respected Washington, D.C. attorney, was chosen by the Justices of the Supreme Court to represent Clarence Gideon. He worked very closely with Gideon.

fall under the Court's ruling in *Powell* v. *Alabama*. After all, that would be a simpler way to help his client, one that did not require the Supreme Court to overrule a past decision.

While Fortas was deliberating, he received a letter from Gideon himself. Circumstances had brought together these two men in their fifties—one a poor prison inmate, the other a successful attorney. Yet Gideon did not hesitate to write to Abe Fortas, asking him what he should do next. Over the next few months, Fortas kept Gideon updated on the proceedings, urging him to be patient. In his September 1962 letter, Gideon told Fortas, "Everything [sic] containing [sic] to my case is of the highest interest to me and everyone [sic] in the prison. And we will certainly welcome all the information about it that is possible."[11]

Fortas asked Gideon to write a letter detailing his life. Gideon's twenty-two-page reply told the story of hardships and past conflicts with the law. At the end, he repeated what he had been saying all along, "There was not a crime committed in my case and I don't feel like I had a fair trial. If I had a [sic] attorney he could brought [sic] out all of these things in my trial."[12]

After reviewing Gideon's materials, Abe Fortas concluded that Gideon did not qualify for an attorney under the special conditions that the Court had laid out in previous cases. He began developing legal arguments for the written brief he would submit to the Supreme Court and for the oral presentation that would follow.

One of the main points in Fortas's arguments was that state courts found it difficult to apply the *Powell* and *Betts* decisions. States and individual judges came to different conclusions when trying to determine if a given defendant was able to represent himself. The ruling was applied inconsistently from state to state and case to case.

As a result, numerous defendants said they had not received a fair trial. They brought their cases to the Supreme Court, which then reviewed and often reversed them. Here Fortas found a good argument to use against those who said that the federal government would be interfering too much in the business of individual states by compelling them to provide attorneys to indigent defendants. When he addressed the Supreme Court at Gideon's hearing on January 15, 1963, Fortas said, "I believe in federalism [giving states some freedom of action], but I believe that *Betts* v. *Brady* does not incorporate a proper regard for federalism." Fortas claimed that when the Supreme Court regularly had to judge what had happened in various state trials, that was more "abrasive" to the states' authority than developing a uniform and clear rule they could follow.[13]

Fortas went on to point out the problems judges had in trying to determine whether a defendant qualified for counsel because of special circumstances. He asked the Court how anyone could expect a judge to conclude by seeing a prisoner: "You look stupid," or "Your case involves complicated facts."[14]

Furthermore, Fortas told the Court, there was a more basic problem with the *Betts* decision, namely "that no man, however intelligent, can conduct his own defense adequately."[15] That conviction lay at the heart of Clarence Gideon's argument. Now it was echoed by Fortas and others who spoke on Gideon's behalf. In his brief, Fortas had noted that "even a trained criminal lawyer will not undertake his own defense."[16] J. Lee Rankin, an attorney with the American Civil Liberties Union who had been Solicitor General of the United States under President Eisenhower, said, "It is time that our profession stood up and said we know a man cannot get a fair trial when he represents himself."[17]

Looking at the Fourteenth Amendment, Fortas discussed the Due Process Clause, stressing in his brief that it "protects one's 'liberty' and 'property' as well as one's 'life.'"[18] That same Amendment promises "equal protection under the law," said Fortas, as he went on to discuss the 1956 case of *Griffin* v. *Illinois*. There, the Supreme Court had held that in light of the Equal Protection Clause, people who could not afford to pay for trial transcripts must be provided with any that they needed for their appeals. In *Griffin*, Chief Justice Warren had said, "We cannot have one rule for the rich and one for the poor."[19]

In affirming this idea, the Court had shown an aversion to economic inequality in the criminal justice system. The poor should have access to attorneys as did the wealthy. Fortas pointed out that most states had already come to that conclusion. As of 1962, all but five states—Alabama, Mississippi, Florida, North Carolina, and South Carolina—had decided to provide counsel to poor defendants facing serious criminal charges.

As he made his arguments, Fortas was aware that the Justices had different philosophies about the incorporation doctrine—the idea that the Fourteenth Amendment incorporates the Bill of Rights and thus they apply to every state. Justice Hugo Black was a strong supporter. Black still firmly believed, as he had said when he dissented in *Betts* v. *Brady*, that nobody should be subject to "increased dangers of conviction merely because of their poverty."[20] Other Justices believed the states should have more discretion to decide these matters by themselves.

Fortas hoped that his arguments would persuade most, if not all, of the Justices to agree on Gideon's case, despite their different judicial philosophies. He later said that because the case had such broad implications, it would help if the Court were as united as possible in its decision.[21]

When Fortas had finished presenting his case, Justice William O. Douglas was so impressed that he called it "in my time, probably the best legal argument."[22] Also supporting Gideon's case were the United States Justice Department and a number of state law officials. Twenty-two states chose to file *amicus curiae* briefs, as "friends of the Court."

Nonetheless, in keeping with the American adversarial system of justice, both sides had an opportunity to be heard. The State of Florida had what it regarded as sound reasons for denying Clarence Gideon's request. Through its attorneys, the state also filed a brief and appeared before the Court to defend its position.

4

The State of Florida Takes a Stand

Just as Abe Fortas and other Gideon supporters found a basis for their views, so did the State of Florida, named as the defendant in this legal action. Bruce R. Jacob, the Assistant Attorney General, bore the major responsibility for preparing and arguing the state's case. His job was to assemble the facts and ideas that would convince the Supreme Court that Clarence Gideon's trial had been properly handled and that he had *not* been entitled to an attorney.

In some ways, it was an awkward position for Jacob, a young attorney who personally believed that poor defendants should be provided with attorneys—though he said states should be free to decide that for themselves. Jacob also said, "My duty is to present to the Supreme Court the strongest possible argument on why the doctrine of *Betts* v. *Brady* should be adhered to. My personal feelings . . . are of no consequence."[1]

In Gideon's case, the State of Florida was confident it had followed the rule of law. As the state's lawyers pointed out in their April 9, 1961, brief, "Petitioner Gideon has made no affirmative showing of any exceptional circumstances which would entitle him to counsel under the Fourteenth Amendment. . . . Petitioner merely acknowledges that he is without funds. . . . The petition contains no allegations as to petitioner's age, experience, mental capacity, familiarity or unfamiliarity with court procedure, or as to the complexity of the legal issues presented by the charge."[2] In other words, during his trial, Gideon had never asked for an attorney based on the special circumstances outlined in the case of *Powell* v. *Alabama.*

The Florida attorneys also pointed out that Gideon had not proven his trial was conducted unfairly nor had he alleged any fundamental injustice or wrongdoing on the part of Judge McCrary or other officials. The state therefore could not be faulted for conducting an unfair trial.[3]

The state based most of its argument on the

precedent (previously established ruling) of the 1942 case, *Betts* v. *Brady.*

Gideon had been tried on a non-capital charge, and the *Betts* ruling only required that poor defendants be provided with counsel in federal cases. Gideon had not been charged with a capital crime and had not faced the death penalty. Unless he were charged with a capital crime, the law as it then existed did not require Florida to provide an attorney at his request.

Knowing that the Supreme Court often prefers not to overrule a previous decision, Florida argued in favor of maintaining precedent, that is, the principles established in an earlier case (here, *Betts* v. *Brady*). Jacob called upon a legal principle called *stare decisis,* which means "to stand by what has already been decided." This well-accepted principle of law has sometimes prevented abrupt or broad changes. Even so, Jacob knew that the United States Supreme Court has been willing to invalidate cases it feels were wrongly decided. The eminent Justice Louis D. Brandeis, who served on the Court from 1916 to 1939, had once said, "The Court bows to lessons of experience and the force of better reasoning."[4]

Like a few other states, Florida had a statute that permitted appointing an attorney for indigents only in capital cases. Jacob knew, as did Gideon's attorney,

Abe Fortas, that some of the Justices supported state rights more than others. Justices Felix Frankfurter and Hugo Black often found themselves on opposite sides of this issue. Frankfurter tended to support federalism, or more independence between states and national government. Black held the opposite view and wanted every state to be bound to uphold the individual liberties found in the Bill of Rights. Jacob argued against imposing a universal obligation to provide attorneys for indigents, maintaining that it went against the separation of states from federal control.

Finally, Jacob discussed the practical problems that might result from overruling *Betts*. He pointed out the burdens on taxpayers and on local attorneys, stressing that some communities lacked the money and enough lawyers to carry out this kind of task. And would the states now be required to provide attorneys for poor defendants even in minor offenses, including such things as traffic violations? he asked the Court.[5]

Others agreed. The Attorney General of Pennsylvania, Frank P. Lawley, Jr., wrote to Jacob, "What worries me most is the possibility that the Supreme Court, if it did overrule *Betts*, would not limit such requirement to felony cases."[6] Those who argued against overruling the Court's decision in *Betts*, including Alabama and North Carolina, wondered about a "socialized" criminal justice system or "criminal welfare program," set up at public expense.

Besides that, Gideon's opponents discussed the negative effects of making such a law apply to prisoners now serving time in jail. Might this not cause a flood of people to come out of prison? As Jacob pointed out, nearly two-thirds of the people in Florida's prisons had not had attorneys during their trials. If the Court overruled *Betts* and made its ruling retroactive, these prisoners could be expected to demand release or new trials.[7] Jacob realized his chances of winning the case diminished in August 1962 when Justice Felix Frankfurter retired from the Court. Frankfurter had supported *Betts*, as well as federalism and less incorporation of the Bill of Rights by way of the Fourteenth Amendment. He was also respected for his intellect and had been a leader on the Court. Nobody was certain how President Kennedy's new appointee, fifty-four-year-old Arthur J. Goldberg, would affect future decisions.

On January 15, 1963, Jacob appeared at the door of the Supreme Court building, sometimes called "the marble temple" because of its elegant and imposing appearance. It was there that he and his opponent, Abe

The United States Supreme Court building—sometimes called "the marble temple" because of its elegant and imposing appearance—was the site of Clarence Gideon's battle for a fair trial with adequate legal representation.

Fortas, along with their respective supporters, made their oral arguments and answered questions from the nine Justices.

During the next few hours, Jacob and Fortas argued their respective positions in terms of the practical issues, as well as the Constitutional questions and the matter of federalism. Was the right to counsel guaranteed by the Fourteenth Amendment? The two men presented their sides of that issue and many others, including whether laypersons could represent themselves effectively at their trials and the merits of keeping versus overruling the decision in *Betts* v. *Brady*.

At one point, Jacob said that, in considering the need for an attorney, the line might be drawn only between noncapital and capital crimes because in the latter people feared the death penalty. Justice Black responded, "Maybe they're fearful of spending years in the penitentiary, too."[8]

When the arguments and rebuttals (counter-arguments) were completed, the nine Justices were left to debate among themselves and ponder the issues raised by both sides. At Raiford Prison, Clarence Gideon and his fellow inmates awaited the Court's decision. The public was expectant, too. Gideon's case had received a great deal of publicity. Americans had read about the case in newspapers and magazines and had their own opinions about the arguments that were presented by both sides. There was more than the usual amount of interest in this particular case. But in the end, it was up to the members of the Court to consider the various arguments and render a decision.

5

The Court Announces a Decision

On March 18, 1963, the Court announced its decision in the case of *Gideon* v. *Wainwright*. As always, the Court was open for visitors who wished to hear the Justices read their opinions. At ten o'clock that morning, spectators in the columned, mahogany-furnished courtroom grew silent as the Marshal of the Court struck his wooden gavel onto a table and announced the arrival of the Justices: "The Honorable, the Chief Justice, and the Associate Justices of the Supreme Court of the United States. Oyez! Oyez! Oyez!"

The Court had voted on Gideon's case during a meeting held three days after oral arguments were presented that January. All nine Justices had finally agreed to rule in Gideon's favor. Two Justices, John Harlan and Tom Clark, had written separate opinions in which they concurred in the result of the decision while expressing individual ideas about some aspects of the case.

Chief Justice Warren had asked Hugo Black, who wrote the dissent in the 1942 *Betts* case, to write the Court's opinion. Black was delighted and later said, "When *Betts* v. *Brady* was decided, I never thought I'd live to see it overruled."[1] According to custom, the Justices read their opinions in the ascending order of seniority. As the most senior Justice to speak that day, Black came last. He began reading the opinion he had written for the Court in the case of number one fifty-five, *Gideon* v. *Wainwright.* After describing the background of the case—Gideon's arrest and the beginning of his trial in Panama City, Black said,

> Put to trial before a jury, Gideon conducted his defense about as well as could be expected from a layman. . . . The jury returned with a verdict of guilty and petitioner was sentenced to serve five years in the state prison.[2]

Black then explained how Gideon had petitioned the Supreme Court, and Black referred to the Court's previous decisions on this matter:

The Chief Justice of the Supreme Court at the time of Clarence Earl Gideon's case was Earl Warren. He is shown here in his office at the Court. Warren asked a delighted Justice Hugo Black to write the court's opinion in the *Gideon* case.

> Since 1942, when *Betts* v. *Brady* 316 U.S. 455, was decided by a divided court, the problem of a defendant's federal constitutional right to counsel in a state court has been a continuing source of controversy and litigation in both state and federal courts. To give this problem another review here, we granted certiorari, 270 U.S. 908. . . . [We] requested both sides to discuss in their briefs and oral arguments the following: "Should this court's holding in *Betts* v. *Brady* . . . be reconsidered?"[3]

Black pointed out the similarities in the two cases—how Smith Betts and Clarence Gideon had both pleaded not guilty, had asked for an attorney and been refused, then tried to defend themselves. Both had been convicted and sentenced to prison (in Betts' case, for a term of eighty years). Justice Black explained that when Betts argued that the Sixth Amendment right to an attorney should be extended to indigent defendants in state courts, "The Court concluded that 'appointment of counsel is not a fundamental right, essential to a fair trial.' . . . It was for this reason the *Betts* Court refused to accept the contention that the Sixth Amendment's guarantee of counsel for indigent federal defendants was extended to or, in the words of that Court, 'made obligatory upon the States by the Fourteenth Amendment.'"[4]

Black then reached the moment Gideon and others had been waiting for as he announced:

We think the Court in *Betts* was wrong. . . . In deciding as it did—that appointment of counsel is not a fundamental right . . . the Court in *Betts* v. *Brady* made an abrupt break with its own well-considered precedents [in *Powell* v. *Alabama* and *Johnson* v. *Zerbst*]. In returning to these old precedents, sounder we believe than the new, we but restore constitutional principles established to achieve a fair system of justice.[5]

Besides precedent, "reason and reflection" led to the Court's decision, said Justice Black, as they looked at these facts:

In our adversary system of criminal justice, any person hauled into court, who is too poor to hire a lawyer, cannot be assured a fair trial unless counsel is provided for him. This seems to us to be an obvious truth. Governments, both state and federal, quite properly spend vast sums of money to establish machinery to try defendants accused of crime. Lawyers to prosecute are everywhere deemed essential to protect the public's interest in an orderly society. . . . Few defendants charged with crime . . . fail to hire the best lawyers they can get to prepare and present their defenses.[6]

In fortifying his argument about the need for an attorney, Black quoted from Justice Sutherland's opinion in *Powell* v. *Alabama*, in which he had said,

Even the most intelligent and educated layman has small and sometimes no skill in the science of law. If charged with a crime, he is incapable, generally, of determining for himself whether the indictment is good or bad. He is unfamiliar with the rules of evidence. Left without the aid of counsel, he may be put on trial without a proper charge, and convicted upon incompetent evidence or evidence irrelevant to the issue or otherwise inadmissible. He lacks both the skill and knowledge adequately to prepare his defense. . . . He requires the guiding hand of counsel at every step in the proceedings against him.[7]

Black claimed that in the United States, people regarded attorneys as essential, "not luxuries," and "the right of one charged with crime to counsel may not be deemed fundamental and essential to fair trials in some countries but it is in ours."[8]

Speaking to the issue of a system of justice that was inequitable for the poor, Black said,

It is intolerable in a nation which proclaims equal justice under the law as one of its ideals that anyone should be handicapped in defending himself simply because he happens to be poor.[9]

As he concluded his remarks, Black mentioned the fact that twenty-two states had joined Gideon's request and asked that the *Betts* ruling be overturned. He declared, "We agree. The judgment is reversed and the cause is remanded to the Supreme Court of Florida for further action not inconsistent with this opinion."[10]

In his memoirs, William O. Douglas, a member of the Court in 1963, pointed out other practical reasons to decide this case for Gideon:

A unanimous Court reversed that decision [*Betts*] . . . not so much because it had changed its mind on constitutional theory but because the failure of defendants to have counsel at their criminal trials resulted in a host of habeas corpus petitions which years later raised constitutional questions that would have been brought up at the trial had the accused been allowed a lawyer.[11]

In *Gideon* the Court did not go so far as to mandate that a lawyer be appointed to defend anybody who might face a possible jail sentence. Some Justices, including Douglas, favored doing so, but Warren believed such a ruling would be too sweeping. The Court left it to the states to decide this for themselves. Warren told his fellow Justices that it was "better not to say [the right to counsel applies in] 'every criminal case' if we don't have to here" but rather to decide Gideon's case alone.[12]

Clarence Gideon heard the news at the Florida State Prison. His fellow inmates crowded around him to offer congratulations and their gratitude. Gideon later told a reporter, "The majority of the men in there with me had been convicted without a lawyer to defend them, and nine out of ten saw a way of getting out if I did."[13]

After the *Gideon* decision, the state of Florida passed a public defender law that required courts to

The "Warren Court," shown here, left it to the states to decide whether or not to appoint an attorney to represent anyone who faced a possible jail sentence. But they did decide in Clarence Gideon's favor at this time. After the *Gideon* decision, the state of Florida passed a law requiring courts to appoint counsel in criminal cases (except when a defendant clearly waived that right).

appoint counsel in criminal cases except when a defendant clearly waived that right. The Alabama and North Carolina legislatures followed. In Mississippi, the courts began a practice of appointing counsel for people in felony cases, while in South Carolina, defendants without attorneys were not allowed to plead guilty. Prison inmates in all these states began filing petitions asking the states to review their cases.

At the time *Gideon* was decided, about 60 percent of all criminal defendants were indigents.[14] In Florida, of 8,000 prisoners, 4,542 had not had the help of an attorney at their trials. As a result of their appeals, the courts found themselves overwhelmed at first with new cases. Staffs worked overtime to handle them. Prosecutors and their staffs had to review the convictions and determine whether there was still enough evidence to convict the accused in a retrial, as well as respond with written briefs to their petitions. Budgets from the counties were strained. Gradually, however, the states developed systems for performing this new function.

As a result of his successful Supreme Court case, Clarence Gideon was retried in August of 1963. Two lawyers from the Miami American Civil Liberties Union (ACLU) offered to defend Gideon in that trial, but he declined their services. Instead, he accepted a court-appointed lawyer who practiced in the Panama City area and knew the place and its people.

The attorney, Fred Turner, did an expert job, pointing out inconsistencies in the testimony of the state's main witness (who later became the prime suspect). Turner spent several days before the trial investigating the evidence and the facts of the case. He found that the main witness against Gideon had told people he "was not sure" he had seen Gideon at the scene of the crime.[15] He urged the jury to consider how odd it was that Gideon did not have much money at the time of arrest, although he had been accused of stealing about sixty-five dollars.

Gideon himself later said, "Everything in the new trial looked the same, the same courtroom, the same judge. But there was a difference. I had an attorney."[16] Something else was different: This time, Gideon was found innocent. After two years in prison, he was no longer #003826. That night, Gideon celebrated by visiting the Bay Harbor Poolroom as a free man.

6

The Gideon Case Today

"You have a right to an attorney. If you cannot afford an attorney, one will be provided for you." These statements, or similar ones, are familiar not only to people who have been arrested but to any American who has watched a crime drama or police show on television. At the time of an arrest, police officers inform suspected criminals of an important right—the right to consult with a lawyer, even if they are too poor to pay for one.

Today, decades after *Gideon* v. *Wainwright*, the right of poor criminal defendants to have a lawyer is taken for granted. Yet until 1963, poor criminal defendants like Clarence Gideon often had to try to defend themselves or go on trial with no defense. Before Gideon's case was decided, many people had the "right" to an attorney only in theory. In practice, poor people had no sure access to legal counsel when accused of a crime. After *Gideon* v. *Wainwright*, the Supreme Court went on to extend the rights of criminal defendants. In *Escobedo* v. *Illinois*, just one year after *Gideon*, the Court ruled 5 to 4 that someone in police custody has the right to an attorney at that time. The right to counsel, they said, begins at such a time "the interrogation is no longer a general inquiry into an unsolved crime but has begun to focus on a particular suspect."[1] Three years later, in 1966, the Court decreed in *Miranda* v. *Arizona* that people must be informed upon arrest that they have the right to counsel, as well as the right to remain silent. Of course, these rights had been present since 1963; the *Miranda* decision mandated that they be made known to those defendants who might not know about their rights.

As a result of these decisions, the Supreme Court and its most visible symbol, Chief Justice Earl Warren, were harshly criticized by many people. They were accused of being too concerned about criminals and "soft on crime," among other things. Yet from 1920 to 1943, Earl Warren had served as a District Attorney and Attorney General of California, where he was known for taking a tough stand against criminals and corruption. He did not view himself as soft on crime, only concerned about equal justice under the law. In his memoirs, Warren later wrote,

> A sizable proportion of the American people, too, groping for a reason for so much criminal activity in our disturbed society but overlooking the root causes for crime—such as the degradation of slum life in the ghettos, ignorance, poverty, the drug traffic, unemployment, and organized crime (often made possible by the corruption of law enforcement officials)—joined in placing the blame on the courts . . .[2]

During the years that *Gideon, Miranda,* and *Escobedo* were decided, law enforcement officers also complained that these rules might restrict their efforts to fight crime and would result in coddling criminals. After the initial uncertainty, many people have changed their opinions. Author Delane Ramsey says, "Recently the chief of police in a major southern city remarked that these decisions have actually strengthened the police. . . . the police have become more professional in the thoroughness and scope of their investigations. The police themselves seem pleased that convictions are now based on hard evidence, not questionable confessions."[3] Law enforcement has also benefited from increasingly sophisticated technology and training.

In response to charges that these Supreme Court decisions led to the pampering of criminals and made it impossible to convict them, a police and courtroom reporter named Richard Deming analyzed some statistics in 1970. He found that about 450,000 people were being charged with felonies each year. Of those, police investigations cleared about 150,000 while some 300,000 others were arraigned (formally accused). After arraignment, about 50,000 did not go to trial because charges were dropped, usually when complainants refused to press charges. (An example of this might be a person who passed a bad check, then made it good.) Of the remaining 250,000, about 220,000 plead guilty, so about 30,000 went to trial. More than 20,000 of them were convicted, while slightly fewer than 10,000 were acquitted.[4]

The 1972 Supreme Court decision in *Argersinger* v. *Hamlin* by the Court under Chief Justice Warren Burger extended the *Gideon* ruling even further, to people charged with misdemeanors (lesser crimes). Justice William O. Douglas wrote for the Court, saying that indigent defendants should have the right to an attorney in all cases in which a prison or jail sentence might be imposed.[5] Douglas also asserted that an attorney should be provided from the time someone was arrested and under questioning, even before final charges were filed.

In 1972, the Supreme Court under Chief Justice Warren Burger, shown here, extended the *Gideon* ruling even further. They granted the right to an attorney to people charged with minor as well as capital crimes.

One author, Bertram Harnett, describes the results of these decisions on the current legal system:

> Outreach of legal service and information to the poor and disadvantaged is a legal priority today. Under the impetus of the famous case, *Gideon* v. *Wainwright* 372 U.S. 335 (1963) indigents in felony accusations are entitled to counsel as a matter of law. This principle has been extended to lesser crimes and to costs beyond lawyer's fees, such as court records.[6]

In the wake of the *Gideon* decision, the new law was applied to inmates who had not been represented by attorneys. By January of 1964, nearly a thousand people had been released from prison.

About five hundred were retried. Hundreds more in various states petitioned for new trials.

A number of reforms followed the decision. According to author and attorney Archibald Cox,

> The new rule set in motion countless local reforms, because the activity of counsel brought to the attention of judges practices that had escaped their notice or that they had let slide, such as confining offenders for long periods without arraignment or advice about their legal rights. The spirit engendered by the decision supplied much of the stimulus for broader undertakings, such as the Attorney General's Conference on the Provision of Legal Services to the Indigent, and the work of the President's Commission on Law Enforcement and the Administration of Justice.[7]

The right to an attorney has been gradually

extended to all of what the Court calls critical phases of arrest and in-custody police interrogation. In *United States* v. *Wade* (1967) and *Gilbert* v. *California* (1967), the Court held that a defendant could consult with an attorney when facing a police lineup for the purpose of eyewitness identification. In *Coleman* v. *Alabama* (1970), it ruled that people had the right to counsel during a preliminary hearing. In *Hamilton* v. *Alabama* (1971), the Court said that people had the right to call in an attorney to be present at the time of an arraignment (formal accusation). A defendant also has the right to counsel for an appeal, according to the decision in *Douglas* v. *California* (1963) and at a posttrial proceeding to revoke probation and parole, as decided in the case of *Mempa* v. *Rhay* (1967).

This right to an attorney is not granted for civil cases, however. When dealing with legal matters in regard to landlords, negligence, debt collection, and so on, indigent people must find ways to get legal help or manage without it.

There are still those who criticize the *Gideon* decision and others the Supreme Court has made with regard to the rights of the accused. During President Ronald Reagan's term of office (1981–1989), the Supreme Court, under Justice William Rehnquist, supported changes in aspects of the law. An editorial in

The 1986 Supreme Court under Justice William Rehnquist, supported changes in aspects of the law following the *Gideon* decision. An editorial in *The New York Times* described the Court's views as accepting in principal the right to counsel but failing to hold lawyers to high standards of performance.

The New York Times described the views of that Court, saying that while they "accepted in principle the right to counsel" they "failed to hold lawyers to high standards of performance—especially in capital cases where the right to a lawyer had been honored the longest."[8] The author went on to say that in some cases it had reviewed, the Rehnquist Court had "excused the ineptitude of defense lawyers and penalized death row inmates for minor missteps by incompetent counsel."[9]

Reagan's Attorney General, Edwin Meese, was among those who said the Warren Court had erred in deciding *Gideon* and certain other cases. Meese said it was not the original intent of the framers of the Constitution that the public bear the expense of covering the legal expenses of indigent people in all situations.[10] Others agree with this idea.

There are still numerous problems in obtaining adequate defense counsel. Across the nation, public defender programs may be meagerly funded. Some critics say public defenders do not spend enough time to investigate their cases and prepare a proper defense. In some places, judges appoint private attorneys to take on public defender cases. Critics contend that when defense attorneys are assigned by the court and paid lower fees (often less than half their usual fees), they may devote too few hours to the case. Their work, while not technically negligent, may be merely perfunctory. They may file fewer pretrial motions. Some experienced defense attorneys say that in cases where the death penalty is at stake, fifty to one hundred pretrial motions are not unusual.

A number of states have fee systems that may contribute to such problems. For example, in Alabama as of 1994, the usual private legal fees started at $125 an hour. In contrast, court-appointed lawyers in capital cases received $20 an hour for out-of-court work, such as interviews and investigations. They were alloted $40 an hour for the initial trial, up to a maximum of $1,000. The state also assumed that attorneys would take no more than one hundred hours to prepare a case.

Some lawyers claim that a hundred hours is not enough to research a capital case. According to Bryan A. Stevenson, head of the Alabama Capital Resource Center, these kinds of fee systems may be "a built-in disincentive for thorough representation."[11]

In an effort to better prepare a larger number of trial lawyers, law schools have stressed criminal law courses more since the time of *Gideon.*

After President Bill Clinton took office in 1993, his Attorney General, Janet Reno, said that she planned to find ways to ensure that defendants have competent counsel in cases in which the death penalty would later be carried out. People who support this idea claim that paying for skilled counsel during trials is less expensive in the long run than the cost of later appeals when a defense had not been conducted properly.

While preparing new anti-crime legislation in 1993 and 1994, the Clinton Administration discussed ways to provide competent counsel for those who might face the death penalty. Other anticrime legislation included gun control, new prisons, stiffer penalties for repeat offenders, and an increase in the number of police officers. The intense debate over these matters shows the continual struggle to find ways to protect people from crime while trying to safeguard the rights of those who are accused of a crime.

And what of the man whose name is most closely associated with the right to an attorney? After his release from prison, Clarence Gideon was no better off economically than before. He was a loner, estranged from his family. From time to time, he worked as an electrician or took part-time jobs on fishing boats in the Gulf of Mexico. He is said to have wept when he received his copy of Anthony Lewis's book, *Gideon's Trumpet*, an account of his experiences and the events that led to the historic 1963 Supreme Court decision.[12]

Author Michael Durham related an incident in

which a young man stopped Gideon in the street and said, "I should thank you. You just got me out of prison." Gideon told Durham, "That made me feel pretty good."[13]

In 1972, a reporter asked Clarence Gideon, "Do you feel like you accomplished something?"

"Well, I did," Gideon told him.[14]

That same year, Clarence Gideon was diagnosed with cancer. Despite treatment at a hospital in Fort Lauderdale, he died of the disease. At his mother's request, Gideon was buried in his hometown of Hannibal, Missouri. The American Civil Liberties Union had a tombstone erected over his grave that includes words from Gideon's letter to the Supreme Court: "Each era finds an improvement in law for the benefit of mankind."

A determined sense of justice inspired Clarence Gideon to call for that "improvement in the law." By seeking justice for himself, he paved the way to a more equitable system for others as well.

Gideon showed that "We, the people" means all of us, not just the rich, the well-educated, the famous, or the powerful. As a result of his efforts, the Supreme Court of the United States took a fresh look at the words inscribed above the columned entrance to the Court: "Equal justice under law."

Questions for Discussion

As the Supreme Court considered *Gideon* v. *Wainwright*,* the Justices faced a number of controversial issues. Other Americans also had a special interest in these issues. State officials, people in all branches of law enforcement, attorneys, and constitutional scholars were among those who took part in lively debates, speculating what the High Court would say and the possible effects of its decision. Here are some of the major issues that were discussed during that time and are still being debated today.

---

* Louis L. Wainwright had become director of the Florida Department of Corrections, so his name replaced Cochran's in Court documents.

1. What makes for a fair trial?

Most legal scholars and other Americans agree that the framers of the United States Constitution intended to guarantee all defendants a fair trial. But just what makes for a fair trial now, more than two hundred years after that document was first written?

When the Gideon case reached the Supreme Court, Americans were looking more critically at the concepts of fairness and justice. More people were aware of social conditions that made it much more difficult for some Americans to have an even chance, not only in the courts but also in education, employment, housing, voting, transportation, and other areas of American life.

Americans are familiar with the words "all men are created equal" and the idea that all are entitled to "life, liberty, and the pursuit of happiness." Yet the civil rights movement of the 1950s and 1960s showed that African Americans did not have equal opportunities. Later, other groups, including Native Americans and women, protested the discrimination they faced in jobs, education, and other areas of life. Throughout the nation, more attention was given to ideas like "equal opportunity" and "equal justice." People searched for ways to make the words in the Declaration of Independence a reality for victims of discrimination.

Along those lines, poverty was seen as a major barrier to equal opportunities. America's leaders discussed ways to meet the basic physical needs of poor citizens and provide access to education and other things that would give them a better chance to reach their potential. People argued that the poor did not fare nearly as well in the legal system as the wealthy. Money bought expert legal advice and gave people much more influence over the outcomes of their trials. The poor clearly lacked access to the same expert help.

Those who believed in equal justice saw major gaps between the trials of poor and rich defendants, from case to case and from one court system to the next. They argued that fair trials could not be a reality unless criminal defendants, whether they were rich or poor, had access to similar resources. This, they contended, was necessary for a trial to be "fair."

Opponents of this idea argued that fairness does not mean providing people with equal goods and services in all areas of life. People cannot afford to buy the same kinds of housing, cars, clothing, health care, or educational services either. Nobody ever expected the government—in effect, the people—to equalize all these things for all citizens. Besides, paying a lawyer was no guarantee of success. Even highly paid lawyers might vary greatly in their skills and success rates.

The counterargument is that affording an attorney for a court trial is a much more serious problem than being able to buy fine clothing or shoes. Defendants are arrested and brought into court at the insistence of law-enforcement agencies of the government, not by choice. Attorneys representing the state are trained and prepared to use every legal means to prosecute the defendant. A poor defense might lead to an innocent person spending years in jail.

For decades before the *Gideon* case, the Supreme Court had tried to define a fair trial. Without specific standards, said Justice Hugo Black, the Court was forced "to roam at will in the limitless area of their own beliefs as to reasonableness."[1] The ambiguity of the Constitution has meant that Justices must do their best to decide what the term *fair trial* means. In searching for answers through the years, the Court began seeking ways local and state courts could be more consistent and predictable in their treatment of criminal defendants.

This coincided with other facts of modern life in America, such as the growth of the mass media and an increasingly mobile population. As people moved from place to place more often and were exposed to the same mass media, regional differences diminished. There was more support for the idea that what was fair in one state should also be fair in another. While states and regions continued to differ in numerous ways, the trend was toward uniformity on matters that involved more basic rights. A prime example was the Supreme Court's ban on laws that forced segregation of the races.

2. Can people conduct their own defenses well, even if they are intelligent and informed?

Closely tied to the concept of a fair trial is the issue of whether people can possibly defend themselves well or even adequately. Abe Fortas and other Gideon supporters pointed out that even an attorney hires another attorney when facing a court trial. In his book, *The Court and the Constitution*, Archibald Cox, a well-known attorney, points out the complex realities of legal actions today:

> Defenses unknown to a lay defendant may be familiar to lawyers. Judges who once had the time and disposition to secure the legitimate interests of a defendant without counsel are now rushed along by overwhelming dockets, the bustling crowds, and dulling tedium of big-city courts. In the circumstances now prevailing, the individual without counsel has much less chance of making a successful defense than the individual who receives sound legal advice.[2]

Some of the services that today's defense attorneys perform for a client include collecting evidence, assessing and trying to discredit the evidence against a client, questioning potential jurors, obtaining witnesses for the defense, deciding whether defendants should testify on their own behalf, and interpreting how various laws and Constitutional issues apply to a case. Attorneys also understand the points of trial law that enable them to object to the tactics of the opposing side.

Could people with no legal training possibly know enough to perform these tasks well on their own? For many Americans, the answer is no. At the time of the *Gideon* case, all but five states had agreed with this stance and decided to provide an attorney for any indigent defendant accused of a felony.

Those who said an attorney was unnecessary claimed that if defendants were having problems with their case, the judge would be there to protect their rights. They also argued that the laws and legal processes carried out in a trial were fundamentally fair, with many built-in safeguards. Defendants could cross-examine the witnesses against them, just as an attorney would. Juries composed of a defendant's peers could be expected to be impartial, taking into account when defendants were pleading their own cases without legal counsel.

3. Does the Fourteenth Amendment's guarantee of due process of law assure criminal defendants of the right to an attorney?

A major element in the *Gideon* case dealt with the incorporation doctrine—the idea that the Fourteenth Amendment was intended to apply the entire Bill of Rights to all the states. Justices had argued about this point for years and would continue to do so after 1963. Justice Hugo Black, who believed strongly in incorporation, had dissented in *Betts* v. *Brady* because he believed the Sixth Amendment guarantee of an attorney should definitely apply to the states, along with all ten amendments.

In a 1947 case, *Adamson* v. *California*, the Court had nearly declared that the Fourteenth Amendment did indeed apply the entire Bill of Rights to all the states. Had one other Justice joined the four who agreed on this, many cases after 1947 would not have come up for review.*

Opponents of incorporation favored a principle called federalism, in which the states have more leeway to decide on some laws and the way they will handle various matters. These people believe the states have

---

* In the years that followed, on a case by case and "right by right" basis, the Court eventually reached the same goal.

their own special circumstances, preferences, and rights and should not be made to follow uniform laws such as one that says they have to provide attorneys for indigent defendants or desegregate their public schools.

When the nation was founded, some of the original thirteen states had feared they would lose their autonomy by joining the Union. The founding fathers and the leaders who followed them had discussed the proper balance between the rights of the states to do things their own way and try out innovative programs against the need for a strong, united federal government that guaranteed certain rights for all Americans.

What is the proper balance? And why should the Supreme Court have the last word in deciding some of these matters? In 1954, Justice Robert H. Jackson wrote:

> In a society in which rapid changes tend to upset all equilibrium, the Court, without exceeding its own limited powers, must strive to maintain the great system of balances upon which our government is based. Whether these balances and checks are essential to liberty elsewhere in the world is beside the point: they are indispensable to the society we know. Chief of these balances are . . . between the central government and the States . . . between state and state; . . . between authority, be it state or national, and the liberty of the citizen, or between the rule of the majority and the rights of the individual.[3]

Ever since our nation was founded, there has been discussion over the proper balance between the right of the states to do their own thing and the need for a strong, united federal government that guaranteed certain rights for all Americans. This question would be addressed numerous times in the United States Supreme Court. The Court is shown here without its Justices. (Photographs of the Court are only permitted when there are no people present.)

During the twentieth century, the Supreme Court became more involved with the liberty of citizens and individual rights. These were years in which the population of the United States increased, and the problems of individuals and their rights were perhaps more in jeopardy than before. Two world wars and the rise and fall of totalitarian governments abroad threatened liberty everywhere. In the 1800s, the Court had focused more on property rights, but in the 1900s, personal liberties—of speech, assembly, religion, and the rights of the accused—took on new importance.

The Court has always dealt only with cases that involve actual people appealing for their rights. So in considering Clarence Gideon's appeal, the Court again demonstrated that interest in balancing the rights of an individual, one who had little power or voice, against the larger society. In considering Gideon's constitutional rights, in view of the Sixth and Fourteenth Amendments, the Court was dealing with a matter that had not been resolved by all the state legislatures. This is often the case, because the interests of elected officials may be geared more toward the majority of citizens than those in the minority, like Clarence Earl Gideon.

Opponents of this view argue that the Supreme Court should not be so actively involved in everyday life and the business of each state. They accuse the Court of legislating morality (making laws about morality issues) and imposing its will against the wishes of the majority. Those who favor the idea of majority rule do not accept the idea that the Supreme Court can protect the rights of individuals and minorities as they have in many twentieth-century case rulings.

4. When does the right to an attorney begin?

As people began wondering if the Court might decide in Gideon's favor, they asked when state courts would be required to offer indigent defendants access to counsel. Should it be at the time of arrest, when one is indicted or charged by police, or at the police station while one is being questioned? Or should defendants be provided with the services of an attorney only during their trial?

Those who believed most strongly in the right to an attorney said that this right should begin at the point in which defendants came under suspicion, even before police began formal questioning. If economic status were not to influence the criminal justice process, then a poor person should have an attorney from the same point as wealthy people would call upon their lawyers for help.

Opponents of this idea raised some of the same arguments mentioned earlier—that goods and services in society cannot be made completely equal for everyone, rich or poor. They also pointed out the practical problems of imposing such a law on every state. Were there enough attorneys to take care of all the cases and were they adequately trained in criminal law?

People also worried that more guilty people might go free and those in prison who knew they were guilty might find ways to get out on a legal technicality. Bruce Jacob, who represented Florida in the *Gideon* case before the Supreme Court, had been chairman of the legal aid clinic in law school. But he, too, expressed concerns about the chance that guilty inmates in Florida would have a way to get out of prison if the Supreme Court ruled in Gideon's favor. He told author Anthony Lewis, "It's easy to think of them [guilty inmates] as heroes, but after you've worked in the attorney general's office you know they're not. They're liars, they're terrible."[4]

Besides that, there would be high costs involved. Counties would have to pay attorney's bills for indigent defendants. Taxes might need to be raised, and much of that money, coming from honest and hardworking citizens, would be used to defend people who were guilty as well as innocent of a crime. This brought up the issue of whether it is right to impose such burdens on taxpayers, since public defenders, the attorneys for indigents, are paid from public funds. Crime in general costs the public a great deal. Besides the costs to victims, taxes are used to fund law enforcement, the court system, jails and prisons to house those who are convicted, and a parole system when people are released. The costs of public defenders add to this burden.

Others respond to this by saying that even if some guilty defendants go free, that is preferable to imprisoning an innocent person. Money is not as important as moral principles, say these people; societies must be judged in terms of how they treat the humblest and least popular citizens as well as the most esteemed. Moreover, as a nation founded on the principle of "equal justice under law," could the United States afford to do less than the most advanced countries? At the time *Gideon* was decided, some nations, including Great Britain, did provide indigent defendants with attorneys. Writing in the *Harvard Law Review* in 1956, Justice Shaefer of Illinois had said, "The quality of a nation's civilization can be largely measured by the methods it uses in the enforcement of its criminal law."[5]

Clearly, there were no easy answers in the *Gideon* case. For every argument on one side, there was a compelling and sincere argument on the other. As it had done hundreds of times in the past, the Supreme Court had to weigh the different viewpoints, balance the rights and responsibilities, and determine what the Constitution required in terms of the right to free counsel.

Chapter Notes

Chapter 1

1. Trial transcript, Circuit Court of the Fourteenth Judicial Circuit of Florida, in and for Bay County, August 4, 1961. Quoted in Anthony Lewis, *Gideon's Trumpet* (New York: Random House, 1964), p. 9.

2. Ibid.

3. Ibid.

4. Ibid.

5. Ibid., p. 10.

6. Ibid., Also Tinsley E. Yarbrough, "Incorporation and the Right to Counsel," in John W. Johnson *Historic United States Court Cases 1690–1990* (New York: Garland, 1992), p. 597. Trial transcripts also quoted in *New Yorker*, April 25, 1964. "Annals of Law: The Gideon Case-I," p. 149.

7. United States Constitution, Amendment VI [1791].

8. United States Constitution, Amendment XIV [1868].

9. Letter from Clarence Gideon to the United States Supreme Court, April 21, 1962.

10. Trial transcript, Circuit Court of the Fourteenth Judicial Circuit of Florida, quoted in Eliot Kleinberg, "Opinion . . . And Justice for All," *Palm Beach Post*, March 13, 1988, 1-E, Also Yarbrough as above.

11. Lewis, *New Yorker,* p. 149.

12. Quoted in David J. Damielski and J. S. Tulshin, eds., *The Autobiographical Notes of Charles Evans Hughes* (Cambridge, Mass.: Harvard University Press, 1973), p. 143.

Chapter 2

1. *Powell* v. *Alabama,* 287 U.S. 35 (1932).

2. *Johnson* v. *Zerbst* 304 U.S. 458 (1938).

3. Bernard Schwartz with Stephan Lesher, *Inside the Warren Court: 1953–1969* (Garden City, N.Y.: Doubleday, 1983), p. 177.

4. *Betts* v. *Brady* 316 U.S. 455 (1942), quoted in Ralph A. Rossum and G. Alan Tarr, *American Constitutional Law, Cases and Interpretation* (2nd ed.) (New York: St. Martin's Press, 1987), p. 437.

5. Schwartz and Lesher, p. 178.

6. Robert A. Liston, *Tides of Justice: The Supreme Court and the Constitution in Our Time* (New York: Delacorte, 1966).

7. Dissenting opinion, *Betts* v. *Brady,* quoted in Rossum and Tarr, p. 437.

8. Bernard Schwartz, *Super Chief: Earl Warren and His Supreme Court* (New York: New York University Press, 1980), p. 458.

Chapter 3

1. Anthony Lewis, *Gideon's Trumpet* (New York: Random House, 1964), p. 66.

2. Ibid., p. 68.

3. Ibid., p. 71.

4. Michael Durham, "High Court's Mind," *Life*, June 12, 1964, p. 86.

5. *Gideon* v. *Wainwright*, p. 338.

6. Bernard Schwartz, *Super Chief: Earl Warren and His Supreme Court* (New York: New York University Press, 1980), p. 66.

7. Lewis, "Annals of Law: Gideon—II," p. 172.

8. Justice M. Harlan Papers, Mudd Manuscript Library, Princeton University.

9. Lewis, "Annals of Law: The Gideon Case—I," p. 158.

10. Schwartz, p. 584.

11. Lewis, *Gideon's Trumpet*, p. 64; Lewis, "Annals of Law: The Gideon Case—II," pp. 142–143.

12. Lewis, "Annals of Law: The Gideon Case—II," p. 148.

13. Anthony Lewis, "Free Defense Put to Supreme Court," *The New York Times, West Coast Edition*, January 16, 1963, p. 8.

14. Ibid.

15. Ibid.

16. Lewis, *Gideon's Trumpet*, p. 135.

17. Lewis, "Free Defense Put to Supreme Court," p. 8.

18. From the brief submitted to the Supreme Court, quoted in Lewis, *Gideon's Trumpet*, p. 135.

19. Quoted in Schwartz, *Super Chief*, p. 193.

20. *Betts* v. *Brady*, quoted in Howard Ball and Phillip J. Cooper, *Of Power and Right: Hugo Black, William O. Douglas, and America's Constitutional Revolution* (New York: Oxford University Press, 1992), p. 222.

21. Lewis, *Gideon's Trumpet*, p. 119.

22. William O. Douglas, *The Court Years: 1939–1975* (New York: Random House, 1980), p. 187.

Chapter 4

1. Anthony Lewis, *Gideon's Trumpet* (New York: Random House, 1964), p. 146.

2. Anthony Lewis, "Annals of Law: The Gideon Case—I," p. 156.

3. Letter to the Supreme Court, April 9, 1961, quoted in Lewis, "Annals of Law: The Gideon Case—I," p. 157; and Lewis, *Gideon's Trumpet*, p. 36.

4. Quoted in Lewis.

5. Anthony Lewis, "Free Defense Put to Supreme Court," *The New York Times, West Coast Edition*, January 16, 1963, p. 8.

6. Lewis, *Gideon's Trumpet*, p. 145.

7. Lewis, "Free Defense," p. 8.

8. Quoted in Lewis, *Gideon's Trumpet*, p. 177.

Chapter 5

1. Quoted in Schwartz and Lesher, *Inside the Warren Court: 1953–1969* (Garden City, N.Y.: Doubleday, 1983), p. 180.

2. *Betts* v. *Brady*, quoted in Rossum and Tarr, *American Constitutional Law, Cases and Interpretations* (New York: St. Martin's Press, 1987), p. 437.

3. Ibid.

4. Ibid.

5. Ibid.

6. Ibid.

7. *Powell* v. *Alabama,* in Rossum and Tarr, p. 472.

8. *Gideon* v. *Wainwright,* in Rossum and Tarr, pp. 473–474.

9. Ibid.

10. Ibid.

11. William O. Douglas, *The Court Years: 1939–1975,* (New York: Random House, 1980), p. 187.

12. Bernard Schwartz, *Super Chief: Earl Warren and His Supreme Court,* (New York: New York University Press, 1980), p. 460.

13. Michael Durham, "High Court's Mind," *Life,* June 12, 1964, p. 86.

14. "The Bar Behind Bars," *Time,* May 22, 1964, p. 88.

15. Anthony Lewis, "High Court Ruling," *The New York Times,* August 6, 1963, p. A-1.

16. Durham, p. 86.

Chapter 6

1. *Escobedo v. Illinois,* quoted in Howard Ball and Philip J. Cooper, *Of Power and Right: Hugo Black, William O. Douglas, and America's Constititional Revolution* (New York: Oxford University Press, 1992), p. 223.

2. Earl Warren, *The Memoirs of Chief Justice Earl Warren* (Garden City, N.Y.: Doubleday, 1977), p. 317.

3. "Lawyer? Do You Want A Lawyer?" In John W. Johnson, *Historic United States Court Cases 1690–1990* (New York: Garland, 1992), p. 602.

4. Richard Denning, *Man and Society: Criminal Law at Work* (New York: Hawthorn Books, 1970), pp. 107–108.

5. *Argersinger* v. *Hamlin* 407 U.S. 25.

6. Bertram Harnett, *Law, Lawyers, and Laymen: Making Sense of the Legal System* (New York: Harcourt, 1984), p. 298.

7. Archibald Cox, *The Court and the Constitution* (Boston: Houghton Mifflin, 1987), p. 249.

8. "Gideon's Promise Still Unkept," *The New York Times*, March 18, 1993, Op-ed page.

9. Ibid.

10. Cox, p. 248.

11. Ronald Smothers, "Court-Appointed Defense Offers the Poor a Lawyer, But the Cost May Be High," *The New York Times*, February 14, 1994, p. A-12.

12. "An Ex-Con Overturns the Law," *Life*, June 12, 1964, p. 87.

13. Michael Durham, "High Court's Mind," *Life*, June 12, 1964, p. 87.

14. Phil Sudo, "Five Little People Who Changed U.S. History," *Scholastic Update*, January 6, 1990, p. 9.

Questions for Discussion

1. Dissent in *Adamson* v. *California* 332 U.S. 46 (1947); 67 Supreme Court 1672 (1947); quoted in Schneyerson, p. 211.

2. Archibald Cox, *The Court and the Constitution* (Boston: Houghton Mifflin, 1987), p. 249.

3. Quoted in Shnayerson, p. 28.

4. Anthony Lewis, *Gideon's Trumpet* (New York: Random House, 1964), p. 185.

5. Justice Schaefer, "Federalism and State Criminal Procedure," *Harvard Law Review*, January 1956, p. 26.

Further Reading

American Civil Liberties Union, Due Process Committee Meeting: Minutes, Tuesday, March 5, 1963 (New York City).

Beaney, W. M. *The Right to Counsel in American Courts*. Ann Arbor, Mich.: University of Michigan Press, 1955.

Belli, Melvin, and Allen P. Wilkinson. *Everybody's Guide to the Law*. New York: Harcourt Barace Jovanovich, 1986.

Bowen, Catherine Drinker, *Miracle in Philadelphia: The Story of the Constitutional Convention, May to September*. Boston: Little, Brown, 1966.

Cox, Archibald. *The Court and the Constitution*. Boston: Houghton Mifflin, 1987.

Cullop, Floyd G. *The Constitution of the United States: An Introduction*. New York: New American Library, 1984.

Denning, Richard. *Man and Society: Criminal Law at Work*. New York: Hawthorn Books, 1970.

Freedman, Monroe H. *Lawyers' Ethics in an Adversary System*. Indianapolis, Ind.: Bobbs-Merrill, 1975.

Friendly, Fred W., and Martha J.H. Elliot. *The Constitution: That Delicate Balance*. New York: Random House, 1984.

Harrison, Maureen and Steve Gilbert (eds.). *Landmark Decisions of the Supreme Court.* Beverly Hills, Calif.: Excellent Books, 1991.

Hyman, Harold M. and William M. Wiececk, *Equal Justice Under Law, Constitutional Development 1835-1875.* New York: Harper & Row, 1982.

Katcher, Leo. *Earl Warren: A Political Biography.* New York: McGraw Hill, 1967.

Kling, Samuel G. *The Complete Guide to Everyday Law.* Chicago: Follett Publishing Company, 1973.

Lewis, Anthony. *Gideon's Trumpet.* New York: Random House, 1964.

Renstrom, Peter G. *Constitutional Law and Young Adults.* Santa Barbara, Calif.: ABC-CLIO, 1992.

Rossum, Ralph A. and G. Alan Tarr (Eds.). *American Constitutional Law: Cases & Interpretation.* New York: St. Martin's Press, 1987.

Schwartz, Bernard. *Super Chief: Earl Warren and His Supreme Court.* New York: New York University Press, 1983.

Schwartz, Bernard and Stephan Lesher. *Inside the Warren Court: 1953–1969.* Garden City, N.J.: Doubleday, 1983.

Simon, James F. *Independent Journey: The Life of William O. Douglas.* New York: Harper & Row, 1980.

Tribe, Laurence H. *God Save This Honorable Court: How the Choice of Justices Can Change Our Lives.* New York: Random House, 1985.

"The Bar Behind Bars," *Time,* May 22, 1964, p. 88 (88–90).

Warren, Earl. *The Memoirs of Chief Justice Earl Warren.* Garden City, N.Y.: Doubleday, 1977.

Westin, Alan F., ed., *An Autobiography of the Supreme Court.* New York: Macmillan, 1963.

White, G. Edward. *Earl Warren: A Public Life.* New York: Oxford University Press, 1982.

Wilson, James Q., ed., *Crime and Public Policy.* San Franciso: Institute for Contemporary Studies, 1983.

Witt, Elder. *The Supreme Court and Individual Rights.* Washington, D.C.: Congressional Quarterly, 1988.

Woodward Bob, and Scott Armstrong. *The Brethren: Inside the Supreme Court.* New York: Simon & Schuster, 1979.

Glossary

acquit—To find innocent.

affirm—To agree that a decision was right and should stand.

brief—A written argument filed in court to support one's position.

capital crime—A serious crime such as murder or rape.

concur—To agree with (as when Supreme Court Justices write concurring opinions).

convict—To find guilty of a crime.

dissent—To disagree with (as when Supreme Court Justices write differing opinions from the majority).

federalism—Separation of powers between the states and the central government.

incorporation doctrine—The idea that the Fourteenth Amendment to the Constitution should make the entire Bill of Rights apply to all the states.

litigant—One who is involved in a lawsuit.

oral argument—Presentation of a case in which one argues a point of view before the Court.

overrule—In the case of the Supreme Court, to disagree with a prior decision and thus revoke it, establishing a new rule of law.

petitioner—One who comes before the Court to plead his or her cause.

precedent—Something that has been previously decided and is then used as a guide for deciding cases that follow.

public defender—An attorney who works for the state in representing defendants who cannot afford to hire a private attorney.

rebuttal—Arguments made to refute a statement or point of view that has been presented.

retroactive—Applying to that which took place or was decided in the past.

remand—To send something back to a lower court for a review of the previous decision.

reverse—To decide the opposite, as when the Court reverses itself on a previous decision.

stare decisis—To stand by what has come before. It is the legal principle of adhering to previously established decisions, or precedents.

writ of habeas corpus—A written order to an official insisting that one has been unjustly imprisoned and should be set free.

Index

About the Author

A native of Ohio, Victoria Sherrow received her B.S. and M.S. degrees from the Ohio State University, attended the Ohio State College of Law, and studied children's literature at UCLA. She is the author of more than forty books for children and young adults, as well as numerous stories and articles. Some of Sherrow's recent books have dealt with public education, mental illness, the U.S. health care system, and the role of the media in presidential elections. She and her husband Peter Karoczkai live in Connecticut with their three children.